THE FIT FACTORS

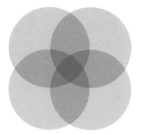

First Edition

Brad Pugh

www.theFitFactors.com

StrengthsPublishing

Strengths Publishing, LLC

Strengths_Publishing_

Strengths Publishing, LLC
2964 Peachtree Road
Suite 510
Atlanta, GA 30305

Second Printing: May 2012

For information regarding special discounts for bulk purchases or customized versions for corporate customers (such as recruiting purposes) please contact orders@strengthspublishing.com

CONTENTS

Online Extras

Download the worksheets shown in this book and more at
http://www.thefitfactors.com/worksheets

THE GOAL

The goal of this book is to level the playing field between you and the companies you'll work for. I want to help you make smart decisions about your next job and your overall career. In doing so, I'll give away some Human Resources strategy secrets used by sophisticated companies. Fortunately, explaining these secrets is a good thing for everyone involved, because everyone wants you to succeed. On the day you are hired, your new manager and company hope that you will be their next "star" – that you'll end up in the right job, performing well, developing at work and helping them grow the business. By becoming familiar with HR strategies, you'll be better equipped to help them get their hiring decisions right and take advantage of the recruiting process they've created.

I've been focusing on how to make the right job decisions for over ten years, from three perspectives: as a consultant, an employer, and as a mentor. Most recently, I've spent the last six years advising HR executives at major corporations on their recruitment, employee performance and retention strategies. Through thousands of meetings with executives, I clearly saw the contrast between employer and employee, recruiter and job seeker, executive and their talented workforce. Prospective employees do not understand what is happening "behind the curtain" when it comes to HR strategy – and if they did, they would be embarrassed at how unprepared they are to manage their own careers.

Second, as an entrepreneur starting my first venture during the dot-com boom, I wanted to figure out whom to hire and how to help my team members succeed. Around that time, I discovered a variety of self-assessments that we could use to help tailor our responsibilities to our unique abilities. My goal was to determine which activities people were naturally better at than everyone else at the office and give them a chance to build their job and career around those things.

Lastly, as a result of my time inside large recruiting organizations and building my own teams, I found many friends and mentees asking me for guidance regarding their own job searches. In those conversations, I tried to learn more about the person's strengths, interests, and goals, with the hope of helping them understand themselves better and search for jobs in a more focused way. Unfortunately, I found that most people did not have a way to figure out what they were good at, what they wanted in a job, and what jobs would best fit them.

The frameworks, diagrams, data and quotes in this book that are the result of hundreds of conversations with managers, executives, mentees, job seekers and individuals interested in connecting what they are good at to what they do at work. Many of the pages had their beginnings as quick lists written over coffee with a mentee or as a grid I drew on the whiteboard as I considered who to hire into my team.

To ensure my observations captured the experiences of a broad group of individuals, I invited others to participate through an online survey. My goal was to capture the experiences of others as I created my recommendations. In fact, I was surprised at how many people responded. During the summer of 2011, my survey invitations went to individuals who visited StrengthsTest.com. In total, nearly one thousand people from over fifty countries participated. Additional details about the survey can be found in the appendix.

Great careers don't just happen. Building a great career requires you to know who you are and what you want and to make a number of key decisions that lead you into great jobs and a rewarding career. Let's begin that journey together.

THE CHALLENGE

DECISIONS MATTER

You're building a career, one job, one experience and one accomplishment at a time.

Careers that thrive and are of great value to the marketplace are those in which each step along the way capitalizes on the previous experience, equipping you for greater success in the future. In other words, strong careers are built intentionally.

If you are striving to build a valuable career, you must recognize the importance of each decision along the continuum.

Each job decision should increase the value of your past and create momentum for the future.

Example 1 – Mary

Past:
Child of military family, lived extensively overseas

Current job:
Intern at defense contractor

Next job:
Government intelligence analyst

Example 2 – Jason

Past:
Architecture student

Current Job:
Commercial real estate agent

Next job:
Real estate developer

Example 3 – Matt

Past:
Account manager

Current job:
HR representative

Next job:
HR consultant

HAPHAZARD DECISION MAKING

There are a lot of reasons to take a new job – but not all of them are good reasons.

At the expense of your career, you might make a job decision impulsively without considering all the factors involved. Things that may initially appear to be good reasons for accepting an offer might be outweighed by the realities of the new job.

While it is impossible to know every aspect of a new job opportunity, a discerning perspective and an intentional decision making process are essential.

We often make impulsive job decisions that undermine our careers.

The First Option

"They said they could use someone starting next week!"

Reality Check: You're a fit because you are available, not because you'll be good at the job.

The Wow Factor

"We can provide you a more senior title and a 10% pay increase."

Reality Check: The 10% pay increase may not be adequate since you'll be working 20% more each day.

The Warm & Fuzzy Feeling

"I met the boss and I really liked her – we'll get along great."

Reality Check: Liking the manager personally doesn't ensure that you will like the job or their management style.

The Escape

"I just have to get out of my current job – I can't take it anymore!"

Reality Check: As long as you are working in a similar type of role or company, you'll always feel this way.

COMPANIES MAKE CAREFUL DECISIONS

In contrast to the haphazard decision process individuals often use, the best companies are systematic in their approach to finding and hiring talent.

Smart companies organize their hiring process around four stages: attracting potential employees, recruiting candidates, screening and interviewing, and making hiring decisions.

Each of these stages is uniquely designed to obtain the greatest number of quality hires for the least amount of time and cost.

Do not be intimidated by this process – after reading this book, you will have an equally impressive process of your own.

Smart companies lead you through an optimized hiring process.

1) Attracting Potential Employees

- **Employment Branding** – identify what people want in a potential employer and job
- **Salary Benchmarking** – determine what to pay by comparing with other companies
- **Targeting** – identify the profile of an ideal person and a strategy to reach them

2) Recruiting Job Candidates

- **Job Posting** – post job openings on company website, on job sites, and to internal network for other employees to distribute
- **Cold-Calling/Emailing** – place calls and emails to potential employees identified in social networks and networking
- **Using Search Firms** – ask a third-party to find potential employees

3) Screening and Interviewing Candidates

- **Screening Resumes** - automated or manual process to find resumes with key skills and experiences listed
- **Screening Calls/Phone Interviews** – initial conversation to determine if candidate is seriously looking for a job, has basic skills, and to verify information
- **Interviewing** – assess the individual for key skills, behaviors, and characteristics that would fit with the company and job

4) Making Decisions and Offers

- **Hiring Decision** – based on factors including: skills assessment, behaviors, "gut feel," personality, etc.
- **Job Offer** – presenting the candidate with the proposed salary, benefits offered, and selling them on accepting the job

COMPANIES DEFINE SUCCESS POORLY

At the end of the corporate hiring process, most companies define success through popular hiring metrics such as time-to-fill a position, cost per new hire, quality of new hire, and retention of the new hire.

While those company-focused metrics are helpful in optimizing a short-term process, they do little to ensure or predict your long-term success in the job or your enjoyment of the new position.

Impersonal metrics quantify success for the companies.

Company's Definition of Hiring Success

- Is new hire still employed 90-days later? ☑
- Is employee as good as the most recent hire? ☑
- Was the time needed to attract, recruit, interview and hire the employee acceptable? ☒
- Was the cost associated with hiring the employee within budget? ☒

STATUS QUO IS NOT WORKING

According to research from Deloitte Consulting, only 21% of workers are planning to stay in their jobs.[1] This means that despite the best intentions of everyone, the hiring process is not working.

People are not just discontent with their jobs, they are looking for new ones. Data shows that individuals who are planning to leave are already active in their job search in some form or fashion.

The bottom line is this: the status quo is not working. Companies are diligently managing their process, but individuals are earnestly looking for opportunities to leave.

Very few people are committed to staying in their current jobs...

Employee's Plans
Are you staying or going?

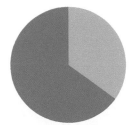

65%
"Leaving"
Employees who have been, plan to, or are currently seeking new employment

21%
"Staying"
Employees who expect to stay with their current employer

... leading to the continuation of the job search.

Searching for a Job
*Are you planning to look for a new employer?**

I have been actively looking for new employment during the past 12 months — 15%

I am currently seeking new employment — 15%

I plan to begin looking for new employment within the next 12 months — 19%

I am passively looking — 21%

Source: Talent Edge 2020, Deloitte Consulting, April 2011
*Survey participants who were actively looking (the first three categories) could choose more than one response.

THE APPROACH OF SMART JOB SEEKERS

In order to overcome the status quo, I will give you a framework for developing your own job search and decision process. I will help you adopt a method for approaching the search, finding job opportunities, interviewing, and positioning yourself for success.

Most job seekers don't have a process like this in place and they don't think systematically

through these questions. As a result, they are left to respond to the activities of companies, allowing those companies to fully drive the job search and decision making

Our focus areas will address all of your key questions.

Key Questions of Job Seekers

The Fit Factors Focus Areas

Key Questions of Job Seekers	The Fit Factors Focus Areas
What factors should I consider when looking at job opportunities?	The Fit Factors Framework
How am I uniquely suited for certain opportunities?	Understanding The Fit Factors
What types of jobs are best for me?	Search Planning
How do I find the best jobs and get in the door?	Job Searching
What should I do in the interview to sell myself and understand if it is the right job for me?	Interviewing
How should I make the decision to accept or reject a job offer?	Decision Making
How can I make sure I succeed in the new job and grow in my career?	Starting & Progressing

TOO MANY FACTORS TO CONSIDER?

Any decision can be a challenge, particularly when there are a lot of different factors involved.

As you evaluate job opportunities, factors such as compensation, company stability, promotion opportunities, travel requirements, and others need to be considered. Figuring out which of these are the most important is difficult.

Even more, knowing how these factors may impact your success and enjoyment of a particular job is likely a mystery.

To make the best decisions, a clear formula or framework is needed. As you'll see on the next page, that is exactly what I've created for you.

With many job factors to consider...

... you need a clear framework.

Company Reputation

Stability

Compensation   Workload   Coworkers

Day-to-Day Responsibilities   Industry Appeal

Promotion Opportunities   Commute

Vacation Time   **?**   Travel Required

Retirement Plan

Manager Personality   Mentoring

Flexible Hours

Training Opportunities

Maternity Leave   Benefits

Growth Potential   Bonuses

**Factor A + B + C
=
Right Decision?**

THE FIT FACTORS SOLUTION

THE FIT FACTORS FRAMEWORK

During my time managing employees and mentoring individuals about their job and career plans, I saw four factors that consistently guided them into the right jobs. Not only did those factors help them make good decisions, but those decisions paid off. They were performing better and advancing more rapidly than those who did not get the four factors right.

These observations, along with my research, led to the creation of The Fit Factors framework which consists of Strengths-Fit, Interests-Fit, Company-Fit, and Goals-Fit.

The Fit Factors lead you to the right job and career decisions.

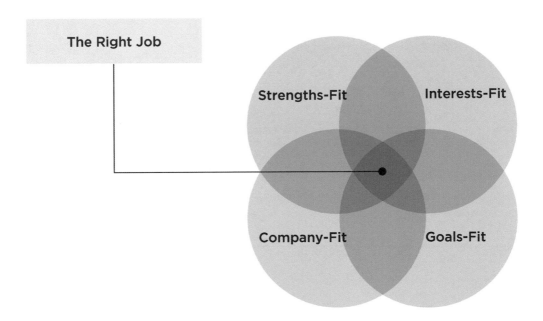

The Fit Factors

Strengths-Fit	**Interests-Fit**	**Company-Fit**	**Goals-Fit**
Does the job/career fit your natural abilities?	Is the work, industry or product/service interesting to you?	Do they provide the characteristics that you are seeking (benefits, reputation, location, etc.)?	Does this help you to accomplish your personal goals (financial, work/life, etc.)?

CLARITY FOR PLANNING AND DECISIONS

The Fit Factors guide your decision making through a series of questions and checklists. By following this process, you can best protect your interests in your job search. Conversely, without a clear framework to evaluate job and career opportunities, you may find yourself relying more on emotion than logic.

For each of The Fit Factors, you will learn how to answer the planning questions and how to use those answers in your planning, search, interview and launch into a new job.

The Fit Factors guide your planning and decision making.

	Your planning questions:	Your decision questions:
Strengths-Fit	What are my strengths?	Will this job use my strengths daily?
Interests-Fit	What are my greatest interests?	Will this job stimulate my interests daily?
Company-Fit	What am I looking for in a company?	Does this employer meet my needs?
Goals-Fit	What are my goals?	How does this job help me reach my goals?

GREAT RESULTS WITH THE FIT FACTORS

The Fit Factors are about you making a good decision and reaping the benefits in your career.

As I asked people about their experiences, I found that when someone had a "fit" the benefits were real and significant for them.

As I compared people with a high-fit to those with a low-fit in their job, I saw that there were more promotions among the high-fit group over the past 24 months. Additionally, the high-fit group also expressed a greater intent to stay in their jobs.

People with The Fit Factors are...

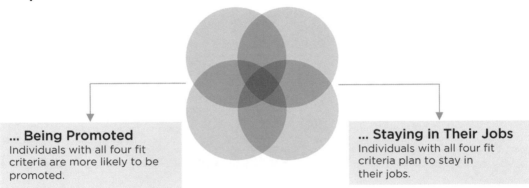

... Being Promoted
Individuals with all four fit criteria are more likely to be promoted.

... Staying in Their Jobs
Individuals with all four fit criteria plan to stay in their jobs.

Recent Promotion
Individuals being promoted in past 24 months

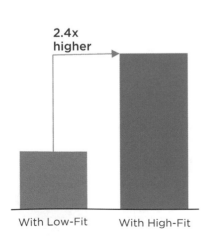

2.4x higher

With Low-Fit   With High-Fit

Intent to Stay in Job
Individuals intending to stay at their job

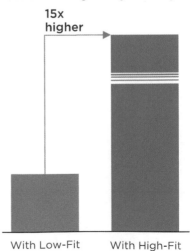

15x higher

With Low-Fit   With High-Fit

High-fit respondents are those with an average of 6.3 or greater across the set of "fit" questions and low-fit have an average of 4 or lower across the "fit" questions. Questions were answered on a 7 point scale.

Source: Does Your Job Fit Your Strengths, Strengthstest.com, June 2011 (789 respondents). See page 65 for methodology.

THE MISSING FIT

In my conversations with job seekers and employees interested in career growth, I saw significant pitfalls when they failed to fit with one or more of The Fit Factors.

Some, lacking a Strengths-Fit, found themselves destined to fail because the core activities of their jobs were not aligned to what they were good at. Others, missing Goals-Fit, were sacrificing long-term career goals for short-term satisfaction.

We've all known people who have been missing one or more of these "fits" at work. They are frustrated, disengaged, and are on the way out of the job.

When you lack fit with one of The Fit Factors, your performance and planned tenure decreases.

Missing Strengths-Fit

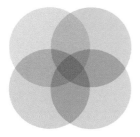

"Destined to Fail"
These people will not become high-performers because their core strengths aren't being leveraged by their current job.

Missing Interests-Fit

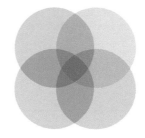

"Misaligned Excellence"
These people are excelling at core parts of their work, but have limited long-term success due to a lack of alignment with their personal interests.

Missing Company-Fit

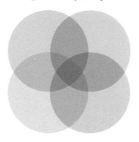

"Right Job, Wrong Place"
These people are doing the right job, but for the wrong company.

Missing Goals-Fit

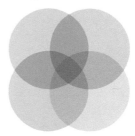

"Shortsighted Bliss"
These people are enjoying their job today, without considering whether it will help them achieve their long-term goals.

UNDERSTANDING THE FIT FACTORS

STRENGTHS-FIT: WHY IT MATTERS

Strengths-Fit is about using your strengths at work every day. I found that 30% of people surveyed had a high Strengths-Fit in their work, and the payoff was significant.

Those with high Strengths-Fit were four times more often at the top of their organizations.

Furthermore, those having a high fit also had stable plans – they were nearly ten times more likely to be staying in their jobs.

Those who are leveraging their strengths at work...

Strengths-Fit

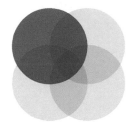

Using Strengths at Work
% of Individuals with High Strengths-Fit

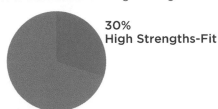

30%
High Strengths-Fit

... have reached the top and intend to stay.

At Top of their Organization
Difference .... individuals at top of organization[1]

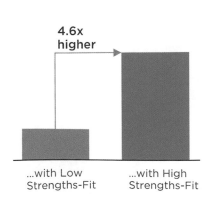

4.6x
higher

...with Low Strengths-Fit
...with High Strengths-Fit

Intent to Stay in Job
Difference... individuals intending to stay at their job

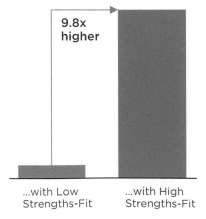

9.8x
higher

...with Low Strengths-Fit
...with High Strengths-Fit

[1] Top of organization means that there is no higher position for the respondent to be promoted into. Typically these are CEO, President, Owner, VP-level positions.

Source: Does Your Job Fit Your Strengths, Strengthstest.com, June 2011 (789 respondents). See page 65 for methodology.

MISCONCEPTIONS REGARDING STRENGTHS

If you are like most people, when asked about your strengths, you probably respond by describing a specific skill or a successful project you were a part of. These are not your strengths.

The success of a project may be due, in part, to a personal strength, but are influenced by other factors such as resources or team members.

Similarly, a specific skill is often of great value, but is only part of a strength you bring to a variety of work situations.

Don't confuse skill and success with strengths.

Two Common Misconceptions

#1) Specific Skills ≠ Strength

Reality:
Strengths require skill, but are not made up of skills alone.

Example Skills:

Project Management Skills

"I've guided a product development team of 15 people through two new products, delivered on schedule."

The Strength:

Organization

Possesses a natural ability to assemble resources, people, and processes to accomplish tasks and/or goals.

#2) Experience ≠ Strength

Reality:
Successes indicate an underlying strength, but should not be referred to as a strength.

Example Successful Experience:

Software Development

"I've been writing software for years and have written a variety of very good programs."

The Strength:

Creative Thinking

Good at viewing challenges through others' eyes and finding creative approaches from scratch.

STRENGTHS DEFINED

Your strengths are a combination of your talents, or natural born abilities, your acquired knowledge, and your developed skills.[1]

Talents are those raw ingredients born into each one of us - the natural ways you think, feel, and act. Adding to talent is knowledge. Knowledge brings facts and experience to inform how you use your talents. Lastly, skills bring the discipline and guidance for you to repeatedly perform strengths.

The key is to operate from your strengths by using your natural talents, building and applying knowledge, and executing with skill at work every day.

Strengths are a combination of your talent, knowledge, and skills.

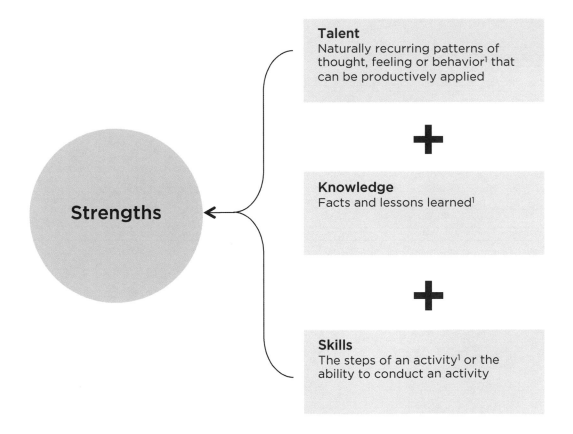

Strengths

Talent
Naturally recurring patterns of thought, feeling or behavior[1] that can be productively applied

+

Knowledge
Facts and lessons learned[1]

+

Skills
The steps of an activity[1] or the ability to conduct an activity

Source: 1) Marcus Buckingham and Donald Clifton, <u>Now Discover Your Strengths</u> (New York, NY: The Free Press, 2001) 29.

You can see the three components of strength when you watch well-known high performers. Their combination of talent, knowledge, and skills created the strengths that led to their success.

Steve Jobs, the late CEO of Apple, built his career as an innovator through his visionary talent, his knowledge of software, and his keen negotiation skills. Ronald Reagan, the 40th President of the United States, leveraged his strength as a communicator, with his training in economics, and his skills as a negotiator to lead through the cold war. Charles Kao, a Chinese scientist, built a career based on his analytical talent, knowledge of optics, and skills in R&D to win the Nobel prize.

People combine their talent, knowledge and skills to accomplish great things.

Example Strength Profiles

	Talent	+	Knowledge	+	Skills
Innovator: Steve Jobs Former CEO, Apple, Inc.	• Visionary • Presenter • Optimizer • Owner		• Hardware manufacturing • Software engineering • Media industry		• Project management • Computer programming • Negotiations
Politician: Ronald Reagan 40th President, United States	• Energizer • Presenter • Rapport Builder • Visionary		• Economics • Sociology • Communications		• Negotiations • Acting • Radio broadcasting
Scientist: Charles K. Kao Nobel Prize Winner in Physics	• Analyzer • Researcher • Self-Starter • Solver		• Microwave and optical technologies • Fluent in English and French • Electrical engineering		• Technical writing • R&D management • Scientific methods

Note: These strengths profiles are hypothetical, for example purposes only.

HOW TO IDENTIFY YOUR STRENGTHS

Identifying your strengths can be done through online assessment tools or informal self-evaluations.

Online assessments such as the VIA Me!℠ or Clifton StrengthsFinder™ will prompt you with questions in a 30-40 minute survey. Upon completion, the assessments provide lists of individualized attributes (talents or strengths)

that best describe you. Self evaluations can also reveal talents through questions like "What do I do best?" or "What has caused me to excel in my work?"

Additionally, it helps you to identify the knowledge, skills, and experience that you bring to your work.

Identify your "big picture" abilities...

Online Assessments

- Clifton StrengthsFinder™
- VIA Me! Profile

Self-Assessment (example)

"I am a natural..."	"... which means that I am..."
Presenter	excellent at communicating information and ideas; visually or audibly
Rapport Builder	great at building relationships with new people
Solver	gifted at problem solving, spotting patterns, and looking into future

... and take inventory of your skills, training, expertise, and work experiences.

Knowledge & Skills (examples)

Management
- Project management
- Budgeting
- Leading meetings

Job/Role Specific
- Fundraising
- DNA analysis
- Data analysis

Computer/Mechanical
- Software (office, graphics)
- Programming languages
- Heavy machinery operation

Training Received
- Public speaking
- Early childhood education

Areas of Expertise
- Commodities trading

Key Experiences
- Start-up business experience
- International work assignment

 See Worksheets section of this book on page 48 and 49 for self-assessment worksheets.

INTERESTS-FIT: WHY IT MATTERS

Interests-Fit is about having your interests aligned with the work you do every day. 42% of the respondents in my survey had high Interests-Fit – and they were succeeding in their jobs.

First, the individuals with high Interests-Fit had been selected for internal or external leadership development programs (typically reserved for future leaders in companies) nearly three times more often than those with low Interests-Fit. Additionally, those with a high fit had six times greater intent to stay in their jobs compared to those with low Interests-Fit.

Those whose interests were aligned to their work...

Interests-Fit

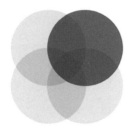

Following Interests at Work
% of Individuals with High Interests-Fit

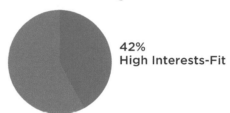

42%
High Interests-Fit

... had been identified as future leaders and intended to stay.

Selected for Development Program
Difference... individuals in leadership development program[1]

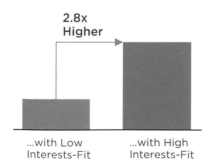

2.8x
Higher

...with Low Interests-Fit   ...with High Interests-Fit

Intent to Stay in Job
Difference... individuals intending to stay at their job

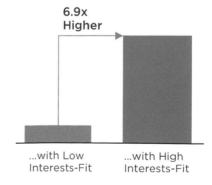

6.9x
Higher

...with Low Interests-Fit   ...with High Interests-Fit

[1] Individuals indicated they have been identified as a leader by their company and are in an internal or external leadership development program.

Source: Does Your Job Fit Your Strengths, Strengthstest.com, June 2011 (789 respondents). See page 65 for methodology.

ALIGNING WORK AND INTERESTS

The key to achieving Interests-Fit is to pinpoint your interest areas and then align those with your job and career.

Do not evaluate your interests in isolation from each other – it is the combination of your interests that will help you to fit some roles better than others.

For example, not all people with interests in science and medicine also have an interest in working with children. Those who have that combination are uniquely suited to fit in a pediatric nursing position.

You are motivated most when you are working in your areas of interest.

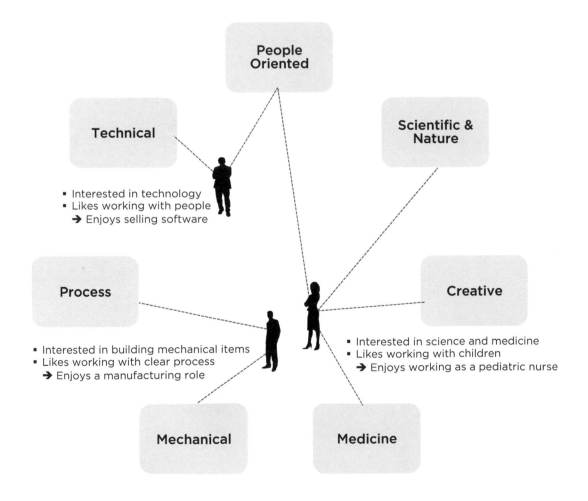

- Interested in technology
- Likes working with people
  ➜ Enjoys selling software

- Interested in building mechanical items
- Likes working with clear process
  ➜ Enjoys a manufacturing role

- Interested in science and medicine
- Likes working with children
  ➜ Enjoys working as a pediatric nurse

People Oriented

Technical

Scientific & Nature

Process

Creative

Mechanical

Medicine

IDENTIFYING YOUR INTERESTS

Capturing your interests can be as easy as a brainstorming exercise. I've identified seven interest categories, you may think of others.

The example below shows a woman who loves to work with technical subjects (like internet technologies) and also enjoys working closely with other people. Knowing this will help her narrow in on jobs that combine hand-on technology skills with interpersonal skills.

Focus on what you do not like as much as what you do enjoy – this will help you quickly rule out a lot of opportunities. In our example below, she can rule out jobs in a hospital or medical environment, even if it is aligned with her technology interests.

Knowing what you are and are not interested in will position you well for Interests-Fit.

Interest-Area	Example:
People Oriented	Meeting new people drives me
	Serving as an expert or helper to others drives me
Scientific & Nature	Working on small (non-political) teams is best for me
~~Processes~~	I do not like created processes or new ways of doing things
~~Medicine~~	I'm not interested in medicine + I get squeamish at hospitals
Mechanical	I enjoy building things and understanding how stuff works
Creative	
Technical	I'm fascinated by new internet technologies like social media
	Reading about technical products in the news and on blogs

 See Worksheets section of this book on page 50 for a blank Interests-Fit worksheet.

COMPANY-FIT: WHY IT MATTERS

You have a good Company-Fit when a company provides the specific characteristics that you are looking for in things such as benefits, reputation, and location.

Only 18% of the people I surveyed had high Company-Fit with their employers, but for those who did, the relationship was mutually beneficial.

Those people with a high Company-Fit had been recently recognized for achievement almost two times more than those with low Company-Fit. The employer also enjoyed loyalty resulting from the fit. Those high-fit employees had nearly seven times greater intent to stay in their jobs.

Those whose company aligns with their ideal...

Company-Fit

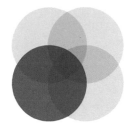

The Right Company
% of Individuals with High Company-Fit

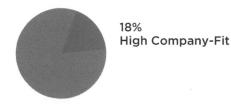

18%
High Company-Fit

... have been identified as future leaders and intend to stay.

Recent Recognition
Difference... individuals being recognized within past 6 months[1]

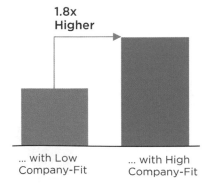

1.8x
Higher

... with Low Company-Fit   ... with High Company-Fit

Intent to Stay in Job
Difference... individuals intending to stay at their job

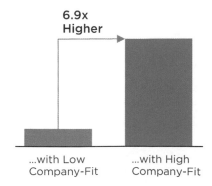

6.9x
Higher

...with Low Company-Fit   ...with High Company-Fit

[1] Individuals indicated they had received positive recognition (such as bonus, promotion, award, positive performance review, or other recognition) over the prior 6 months.

Source: Does Your Job Fit Your Strengths, Strengthstest.com, June 2011 (789 respondents). See page 65 for methodology.

A COMPANY'S VALUABLE CHARACTERISTICS

In order to make good job and career decisions, you will need to understand and evaluate a variety of key company characteristics. Becoming familiar with these characteristics will allow you to see positive and negative aspects before you experience them as an employee.

Smart companies manage these characteristics. They actively evaluate themselves and make decisions regarding how they want to position themselves relative to other companies.

There are a large number of characteristics that can make a company an ideal place to work.

Characteristics by category

Health Benefits	• Company offered insurance • Family coverage options • Paid sick leave	• Maternity coverage • Maternity/Paternity leave
Location/ Commute	• Transportation options (subway, car, walk) • Free parking	• Work from home options • Office amenities (private office, fitness center, cafeteria, etc.)
Management	• Tenure of executive • Leadership track-record	• Industry experience of leadership team
Training	• Formal training programs offered • Orientation/onboarding program • Mentoring programs	• Education reimbursement allowance • Online training available
Career Opportunities	• Time-in-job requirements prior to promotion or transfer • Formal career paths specified	• Cross-functional assignments offered • Job rotations encouraged • Internal job postings available
Reputation	• Recognition as industry leader • Positive product/service reputation • Value of company to your resume	
Pay/Salary Levels	• Published pay levels for jobs • Clear company pay philosophy • Bonuses available and achievable	• Annual base pay increases (%) • Pay for performance incentives
Supervisor	• Amount of experience managing teams • Track record promoting team members	• Turnover on teams (fired, promoted, quit)

You will be at a great advantage by deciding what items are important to you in a company, and comparing potential employers against those items. Companies can differ greatly.

For example, many companies decide to attract talent by paying employees more generously than their competitors. Others pay modestly and make up for it with rich training opportunities.

You will not find this information by simply viewing their website, or through a quick conversation with recruiters. Uncovering this detail will require you to proactively look for information online (at sites such as theVault.com or Bloomberg.com), through questions during the recruiting process, and seeking perspectives from existing employees.

Understand the characteristics of each employer so that you can assess their strengths and weaknesses.

	Alpha Corp.	**Beta Corp.**
Health Benefits	Full, including maternity	Limited, but health savings account
Location/ Commute	45 minutes (heavy traffic), $70 parking/mo.	15 minutes, free parking
Management	Very experienced leadership team, involved in community boards	New to industry and company, positive reputation
Training	Two weeks onboarding/ orientation, ~20 hours training/year	Three days orientation, lots of on-the-job, external training as needed
Career Opportunities	Typical 18-months until promotion, two good career paths	Quick promotions for high-performance (6+ months), fast growing... many potential paths
Reputation	Conservative, excellent product reputation	Entrepreneurial, not well known
Pay/Salary Levels	Pay is typical for positions	Pay lower than market rates, heavy focus on bonuses
Supervisor	Experienced, formal style, 10 years experience / managing teams	Very smart, two years management experience, good rapport

 See Worksheets section of this book on page 51 for a blank Company-Fit worksheet.

GOALS-FIT: WHY IT MATTERS

By achieving Goals-Fit you will position yourself to accomplish the things that are important to you over the long-term, such as your financial goals, work/life balance, and career aspirations.

While I found relatively few people in my survey who believe they are well positioned to accomplish their goals, those who were saw resoundingly positive results.

More of these high Goals-Fit individuals had been recently promoted than those with low Goals-Fit, and they indicated they were six times more likely to stay in their jobs.

For those in jobs that were helping them achieve goals...

Goals-Fit

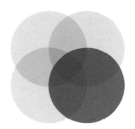

Achieving Goals through Work
% of Individuals with High Goals-Fit

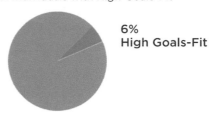

6%
High Goals-Fit

... their promotion rates and plans to stay were elevated.

Recent Promotion
Individuals being promoted in past 24 months

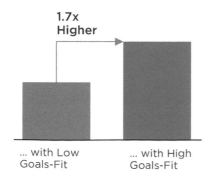

1.7x
Higher

... with Low Goals-Fit   ... with High Goals-Fit

Intent to Stay in Job
Difference... individuals intending to stay at their job

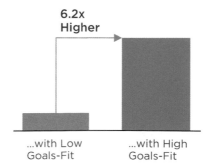

6.2x
Higher

...with Low Goals-Fit   ...with High Goals-Fit

Source: Does Your Job Fit Your Strengths, Strengthstest.com, June 2011 (789 respondents). See page 65 for methodology.

THE IMPORTANCE OF GOALS

Without identifying your long-term goals, it will be impossible to find the right Goals-Fit. Goal planning for your job search needs to focus on career, financial, and work/life goals.

I recommend that you create a goal for each category, then work backward to determine the path to reach that goal. This will help you see which opportunities make sense for you.

For example, if your goal is to become a CEO of a company, you will plot a series of steps that will prepare and position you for that goal. If your primary goal is to spend more time with family and friends, then a high paying job with travel half the year may not be the best fit.

Goals determine your direction, activities, and destination in life.

Career Oriented Goal

Business Analyst — MBA Degree — Regional Sales Manager — VP of Sales — Goal: *CEO of a Public Company*

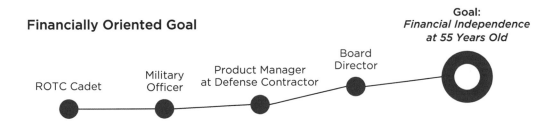

Financially Oriented Goal

ROTC Cadet — Military Officer — Product Manager at Defense Contractor — Board Director — Goal: *Financial Independence at 55 Years Old*

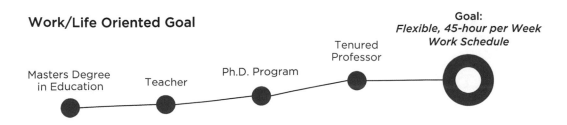

Work/Life Oriented Goal

Masters Degree in Education — Teacher — Ph.D. Program — Tenured Professor — Goal: *Flexible, 45-hour per Week Work Schedule*

IDENTIFYING YOUR CAREER GOALS

Setting your goals is the first step in achieving them. As you think about your work, it is important that you understand how your work will help you achieve your career, financial, and work/life goals.

When planning your career goals, consider whether you'd like to manage teams or become a specialist who is not responsible for people.

With your financial goals, set both short- and long-term objectives. Finally, your work/life goals should be based on an ideal week or month.

A note for the indecisive: setting goals sooner gives you more time to accomplish them!

Career aspirations, financial achievement, and work/life balance need to align to a job or career opportunity.

Career-Fit Goals: (examples)

> **Career**
>
> - I'd like to become an expert in my field.
> - I want to be a hands-on specialist, rather than a manager who delegates work to others.
> - I'd like to mentor people in my field and company.
> - I want to always work for a big company where I can rise through the ranks and be responsible for a product, and have them pay for training every year.

> **Financial**
>
> - I'd like to make $10k more per year within 2 years. I'd like to earn $100k per year by the time I'm 40.
> - I want to save enough for my kids' college tuition by the time they are 15 years old.
> - I'd like to be able to afford an away vacation every year.

> **Work/Life Balance**
>
> - I want to average between 40-45 hours per week (never more than 60 hours in a given week).
> - I want to have the opportunity to travel for business a few times per year.
> - I'd like to have at least 3 weeks vacation per year by the time I am 40.
> - I need my schedule to allow me to coach my son's soccer team each fall (leave the office by 3:30).

  See Worksheets section of this book on page 52 for a blank Goals-Fit worksheet.

POSITIONED TO FIT

Understanding The Fit Factors and your unique strengths, interests, ideal company characteristics, and personal goals now puts you in a position to search for and identify the right job opportunities.

Capturing the key elements from each of the "fits" will keep you focused on what is important as you start your search.

Guide your job decisions and career with a synopsis of your fit.

Strengths-Fit

"I am a natural..."

- Presenter
- Problem solver
- Organizer

"My essential knowledge and skills are..."

- Budgeting
- Project management
- Internet technologies

Interests-Fit

"My interests are in..."

- Technology
- Building things
- Meeting new people
- Serving as an expert to others

Company-Fit

I am looking for the following in a company:

- Excellent family healthcare coverage
- Less than 30 minute commute
- Experienced managers
- Excellent training opportunities
- Career growth opportunities

Goals-Fit

My career, financial, and work/life goals are:

- Become an expert in my field
- Earn $100k per year soon
- 40-45 hour work week, flexible schedule to occasionally leave at 3:30 pm

 See Worksheets section of this book on page 53 for a blank "Positioned to Fit" summary worksheet.

TAKING ACTION

CREATING YOUR CAREER PLAN

There are many roles and industries from which you can choose to build a career. Finding the roles and industries that are well suited to your strengths helps accomplish the goal of finding and thriving in a job.

To identify potential job and career paths, you need to review your strengths and interests alongside a list of potential jobs.

To help you do this, I have created a chart that lists the jobs and industries of my survey participants, organized based on their strengths themes in the Appendix.

Once you know your Fit Factors, you can identify roles and industries for your search.

Your Fit Factors Determined

Identify Your Potential Paths

Example Strengths

Presenter
Visionary

Example Interests

Technical
People Oriented

Strengths & Interests Matching Job Roles

Strengths and interests can be utilized in any role or industry, but some jobs and industries are better suited to you.

Job Role (examples)	Yes	Maybe	No
Account Management	☐	☑	☐
R&D/Scientific	☐	☑	☐
Sales	☑	☐	☐

Job Industry (examples)	Yes	Maybe	No
Accounting	☐	☐	☑
Advertising	☐	☑	☐
Biotech	☑	☐	☐

 See page 60 of the appendix for Strengths Matching Job Suggestions by work area and industry from the survey participants

 See Worksheets section of this book on pages 54 and 55 for a blank Job Role and Industry Interests worksheets

THE BEST SOURCES FOR JOBS

To be a smart job seeker, be aware that relying on online job boards (such as Monster, JobStreet, or SimplyHired) is not your best source. As of June 2011, there were 3.7 million job openings on SimplyHired.com, yet most new hires are made through employee referrals.[1,2] While companies post jobs online, they prefer to hire through their existing employees. That means that the best way for you to learn about opportunities is through your personal and professional network. This allows you to utilize their experiences and relationships to learn about opportunities and get inside information. Any recruiter will tell you that referrals get top priority and consideration in the recruiting process.

The best way to search for a job and get hired is through the people you know.

How People Find Jobs and Get Hired
2010 Sources of Hire[2]

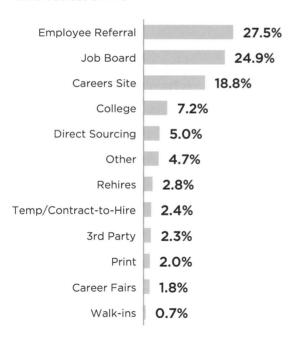

Employee Referral	**27.5%**
Job Board	**24.9%**
Careers Site	**18.8%**
College	**7.2%**
Direct Sourcing	**5.0%**
Other	**4.7%**
Rehires	**2.8%**
Temp/Contract-to-Hire	**2.4%**
3rd Party	**2.3%**
Print	**2.0%**
Career Fairs	**1.8%**
Walk-ins	**0.7%**

Cast a Wide Net
The Most Frequent Sources of Job Referrals

- Friends
- Faith-based communities
- Prior co-workers
- Alumni organizations
- Neighborhood groups

How-To Network for Referrals

Online
Use LinkedIn, Facebook, and college alumni directories to find contacts who work in roles and industries you are focusing on.

In-Person
Rather than simply asking for a referral, ask individuals for advice or information about their role and experiences within that company or industry. They may offer a referral if appropriate.

Source: 1) "US National Job Trends," Simply Hired Inc., June 2011 <http://www.simplyhired.com/a/trends/national> 2) Gerry Crispin and Mark Mehler, "10th Annual CareerXRoads Source of Hire Report," CareerXRoads, March 2011 <http://www.careerxroads.com/news/SourcesOfHire11.pdf>

THE FIT FACTORS IN AN INTERVIEW

Traditionally, companies conduct 99% of the questioning during an interview. They are focused on learning as much as they can about you as a potential employee.

With a bit of preparation, you can sell yourself effectively in the interview and, just as important, equip yourself to make a smart decision about the job using The Fit Factors.

To do this, describe yourself clearly, explaining your talents, knowledge, and skills, then ask questions about the strengths needed for the job and the company's characteristics.

Sell yourself by explaining your strengths...

You Describe Your Strengths

Talents
Explain your talents in terms that the interviewer will understand and can apply to the job.

Examples:
Achiever® (StrengthsFinder® theme)
"I would describe myself as a high-achiever - this means I have a personality that needs to check things off and get things done. I typically take on a lot of work, voluntarily, and enjoy plowing through it. The downside is even at home, when I'm not working, I have to be checking things off."

Researcher
"I'm really good at studying vast amounts of information and gaining a quick understanding of the material so I can explain it to others or use it to make decisions. In technology, I've used this to stay on top of mobile computing trends."

Knowledge & Skills
Connect your knowledge and skills to your talents.

Example:
iPhone App Developer
"An area where I've built knowledge and skills in the last year is in iPhone app development. I was able to quickly learn some basics and build a simple app in my spare time."

 See Worksheets section of this book on page 56 for a blank Interview Notes worksheet

... and assess the opportunity by asking smart questions.

They Answer Your Smart Questions

Uncover Strengths Needed
Ask the interviewer questions that will reveal the type of strengths and experiences top performers in the job have.

Example Strengths-Fit Questions:
- *What are some characteristics of the best people doing this job?*
- *What factors have led people to fail in this role?*

Learn about the Company & Goals
Assess whether the company is a fit with your ideal workplace by asking questions.

Example Company-Fit Questions:
- *Training – "Is there any training provided for someone stepping into this role? What training options might there be over the first few years in the role?"*
- *Career Opportunities – "Can you describe the typical career progression for someone in this role?"*
- *Supervisor – "Tell me about the work and management experience of the supervisor for this position."*
- *Pay Levels (ask HR only) – "What is the company-wide pay strategy relative to other companies – pay below, at, or above market rates?"*

Example Goals-Fit Question:
- *Work/Life – "What are the typical hours, travel and after work/weekend expectations for this role?"*

MAKING A DECISION

At this point in your decision process you are ready to choose using The Fit Factors.

In the example below, I've provided sample strengths, interests, goals, and company preferences, and indicated the fit with each by selecting the appropriate checkbox.

After answering each section for yourself using the blank worksheet on page 57, you'll be equipped to make a decision based on your unique profile.

You can also add up your answers to provide a total score for the opportunity and for comparison with other opportunities.

"Does this job fit my..."

Strengths	Yes	Partially	No	Notes:
Strength 1: Rapport-builder	☑	☐	☐	—Meet many new clients each month
Strength 2: Self-Starter	☐	☑	☐	—Project ownership opportunities
Strength 3: Owner	☐	☑	☐	—Knowing the competition will be key
Strength 4: Presenter	☑	☐	☐	—3+ weekly presentations

Goals	Yes	Partially	No	Notes:
Career: Entrepreneur	☐	☐	☑	Big company ☹
Financial: $750k at 45	☐	☑	☐	Hitting MBOs each year means good bonuses
Work/Life: Done at 5 pm	☐	☑	☐	Lots of travel

Interests	Yes	Partially	No	Notes:
Interest 1: Technology	☑	☐	☐	Yes – high-tech company!
Interest 2: Meeting people	☑	☐	☐	Client facing role
Interest 3: Learning new things	☑	☐	☐	Lots of new product releases

Company Preferences	Yes	Partially	No	Notes:
Health Benefits	☑	☐	☐	Maternity covered
Location/ Commute	☑	☐	☐	20 minutes max
Management	☐	☐	☑	Very young managers
Training	☐	☐	☑	Training geared for entry-level
Career Opps	☐	☑	☐	
Reputation	☑	☐	☐	
Pay Levels	☐	☑	☐	Average pay
Supervisor	☐	☐	☐	Haven't met

See Worksheets section of this book on page 57 for a Job Decision worksheet

Total Score (optional): __8__ Yes __6__ Partial __3__ No

GETTING A QUICK START ON THE JOB

As with any big decision, there are risks involved. According to consultants, half of newly hired employees quickly fail or leave the job.[1,2]

After making an informed decision about a job, a large part of your success will be based on your "onboarding" experience at the company.

Specifically, getting "onboarded," as HR gurus like to call it, means three things: asking your manager for clear expectations, getting feedback (soon and often), and finding a mentor or coach to help you as you adapt to the new job, manager, and team.

There are risks in taking on a new job that can be reduced by being intentional about the way you get started at the job.

Risks After Starting a New Job
Senior-Level Hires Failing within 18 Months[1]

50%
Fail in Job

Hourly Workers Leaving within First 120 Days[2]

50%
Leave Job

Solving Challenges Though "Onboarding"
Benefits of Quality Onboarding

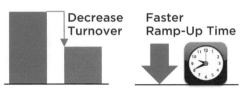

Decrease Turnover   Faster Ramp-Up Time

Quickly and Successfully Getting "Onboarded"

Set Expectations -
Ask your manager for clear expectations for your work. If possible, ask for examples and measures of success.

Seek Feedback -
Approach your manager within the first three weeks to ask for feedback on your work. Insist on two things that you've done well and two things that could be improved.

Find a Mentor, Coach, or Friend –
Identify someone other than your manager to answer your questions. Look for someone who knows a bit about the job, culture, and products/services to rely on for guidance. Consider asking your manager to arrange such a relationship for you.

Source: 1) Smart, B. (1999). Topgrading: How leading companies win by hiring, coaching, and keeping the best people. 2) Krauss, A. D. (2010). Onboarding the hourly workforce. Poster presented at the Society for Industrial and Organizational Psychology (SIOP), Atlanta, GA.

DEVELOPING YOURSELF AT WORK

Building a successful career requires continued development of your talent, skills, and knowledge. Getting that development should come from your on-the-job experiences more than through the traditional "training" options many people rely on.

Learning gurus describe this emphasis toward on-the-job learning as the 70-20-10 Model of Development.[1] The numbers 70-20-10 represent the percentage of learning that should be achieved through your job, relationships, and training.

Don't expect managers or your company to get this right – seek out your own opportunities to develop.

Seek to grow and develop every day, primarily through your work, and occasionally through relationships and training.

Where We Learn
The 70-20-10 Model of Development[1]

70%
On-The-Job

The biggest opportunity for learning comes from our day-to-day work. View your work and projects not simply as doing your job, but as opportunities to grow and learn.

Before, during, and after you undertake an activity, ask yourself: "What can I learn from this experience and how will I use this learning again?"

Examples:

- Spearhead a new technology initiative
- Train new or promoted co-workers
- Manage a new project

20%
Relationships

The people inside and outside your office should be a significant source of learning. Someone with skills and experience in an area of interest can offer you a great learning opportunity.

Examples:

- Find an expert in your area of work
- Discuss best practices with co-workers

10%
Training

A small portion of your development should come from training. Look only for training that provides skills that can't be learned anywhere else.

Examples:

- Attend a training class
- Join a webinar/online course
- Read strategy or how-to books

Source: 1) Lombardo, Michael M. and Robert W. Eichinger, Preventing Derailment: What to Do Before It's Too Late, Center for Creative Leadership Press, 1989)

MOVING UP (OR OUT)

Making a decision to start a specific job using The Fit Factors is only the starting point. Building a strong career is a process that requires ongoing effort and reflection.

Your aim should be for your strengths, interests, goals, and company to fit more and more over time.

This will require you to actively observe your progress and look for opportunities around you. Some individuals take time every 90 days to do this, while others are always doing it informally.

The key is that your career is yours to own, and you'll have yourself to thank for your progress.

Actively manage your career so that you are moving toward your strengths, interests, goals, and ideal company.

Your Goal: Increasing Fit
Improvement of Fit Over Time at Work

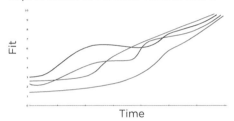

You Own Your Career

"While the company can certainly help move people along in their careers, employees need to understand that only they have their best interests in mind... they are their own best advocates for their career."

- Human Resources Executive

Your Strategy: Look for Opportunities

Strengths
- Which parts of my job are most utilizing my strengths?
- Can I specialize my job to do more of the things that leverage my strengths?
- What roles do I see that appeal to my strengths?
- Where can I use my strengths outside my job?

Company
- How well does this satisfy my ideal for an employer?
- What are the top three other firms for my role and interests and how do they compare to my ideal employer?

Interests
- What products, services or roles are most interesting in my company? At other companies?
- Are there new technologies, roles and/or industries that better suit my interests that I should investigate?

Goals
- How is my job positioning me for my career goals? Is it time to step into a role further along my progress plan?
- What opportunities exist that could significantly improve my finances?
- What work/life trade-offs would I make if I moved into a new role?

CONCLUSION

The average person surfs the web looking for interesting jobs and submits dozens of resumes, only to hear back from a few prospective employers. They make their best efforts in the interviews and ultimately accept a job, hoping they made the right decision.

Hope is not a strategy. The Fit Factors framework is.

I've shared with you The Fit Factors, which I've found to have a meaningful impact on success. The Fit Factors framework will help you narrow in on what matters for you and what opportunities will allow you to succeed based on your strengths, interests, goals, and company preferences. Not only will your decisions be clearer and better informed, but you'll likely experience greater success at work and find yourself committing to stay in that job longer than most individuals who lack fit with their job.

You also have insider information on how companies and their HR organizations operate and think about you as a potential hire and as an employee. As a result, you'll know where you are in their process, how they are positioning themselves and how to get referred to find out about and interview for opportunities. Even after you get the offer, you'll set yourself up for success by seeking out the help you need - starting your first day on the job - and you'll proactively find ways to grow and develop.

As you use the The Fit Factors from this book, I'd like to continue the conversation with you. When you make decisions, tell me about that decision and what happened, whether you changed jobs, companies or rededicated yourself to your current career path. Simply go to www.TheFitFactors.com/DecisionMade and tell me your story.

WORKSHEETS

Online Extras

Download additional copies of these worksheets and more at
http://www.thefitfactors.com/worksheets

Identifying your strengths can be done through online assessment tools or informal self-evaluations.

Online assessments such as the Clifton StrengthsFinder™ and the VIA Me! Profile ask you 30-40 minutes of online surveying. After completing the online questions, the assessments provide lists of attributes (talents or strengths) that describe you.

Self evaluations can also reveal talents through questions like "What do I do best?" or "What has caused me to excel in my work?" A list of potential talents and a self evaluation is provided below and on the next page.

Q: What type of "big picture" abilities do I have?

"I am a natural...." **"... which means that I am..."**

☐ Coach	great at encouraging and seeing potential in people
☐ Competitor	skilled at accomplishing goals, especially when opportunities to rank ahead of goals and others is possible
☐ Connector	gifted at helping establish relationships between others based on shared interests or needs
☐ Counselor	easily able to detect others feelings and understand individual needs
☐ Energizer	excellent at bringing energy to situations and teams, leveraging an optimistic outlook
☐ Fosterer	great at managing and building deep relationships with friends, clients, and partners
☐ Initiator	gifted at taking action without stalling or delay
☐ Optimizer	excellent at seeing the potential for improvement and pushing for progress
☐ Organizer	excellent at assembling resources, people, and processes to accomplish tasks or goals
☐ Owner	excellent at proactively taking ownership of situations and seeing them through to completion
☐ Presenter	excellent at communicating information and ideas, visually or audibly
☐ Rapport Builder	great at building relationships with new people
☐ Reconciler	gifted at resolving tensions with people, by finding common ground or guiding them through difficult situations
☐ Researcher	excellent at gathering information, connecting ideas, and applying to work
☐ Self-Starter	restless to accomplish things daily, very hard working
☐ Solver	gifted at problem solving, spotting patterns, and looking into the future
☐ Thinker	great at making comprehensive assessments (often with data) and analyzing risk and reward
☐ Visionary	a great creative energy source for big, new ideas

WORKSHEET TO CAPTURE YOUR STRENGTHS

To equip yourself to make successful job and career decisions based on The Fit Factors, use the template below to list the items that build and contribute to your strengths.

Included in the worksheet are components that support your strengths, such as specific training you've received and key experiences

where you've built knowledge, skills, and strengths.

Keep in mind that, depending on where you are in your career, you may not yet have specific management or technical skills. Additionally, specific areas of expertise may not have been built for you.

Q: What skills, training, expertise, and experiences do I have that I like to use for work?

Knowledge & Skills

Management	*Job/Role Specific*	*Computer/Mechanical*
▪	▪	▪
▪	▪	▪
▪	▪	▪
▪	▪	▪
▪	▪	▪
▪	▪	▪
▪	▪	▪
▪	▪	▪
▪	▪	▪
▪	▪	▪
▪	▪	▪
▪	▪	▪

Training Received	Areas of Expertise	Key Experiences
▪	▪	▪
▪	▪	▪
▪	▪	▪
▪	▪	▪
▪	▪	▪
▪	▪	▪
▪	▪	▪

To equip yourself to make a job and career decision based on The Fit Factors, use the template below to note your interests and provide examples.

Circle the interest areas that describe you best. Add additional interest areas as needed at the bottom.

Q: I'd find my work most interesting if I were focused on or working with... (choose and list below)

Interest Area

People Oriented
_____
_____
_____

Scientific & Nature
_____
_____
_____

Processes
_____
_____
_____

Medicine
_____
_____
_____

Mechanical
_____
_____
_____

Creative
_____
_____
_____

Technical
_____
_____
_____

To prepare for a job and career decision using The Fit Factors, you will find below a list of eight important characteristics to consider in a company.

To capture your needs and wants separately, note your "minimum" requirement for each and then your "ideal." Finding a company that offers your ideal in all items may not be realistic, but identifying what you would like to have and noting it when you find it will serve you well in your decision making process.

Q: What is important to you in an employer?

	What is your minimum requirement?	*What is your ideal?*
Health Benefits		
Location/ Commute		
Management		
Training		
Career Opportunities		
Reputation		
Pay/Salary levels		
Supervisor		

Note: some of the items above may not be important for you. If so, write N/A in the corresponding row.

Setting your goals is the first step in achieving them.

Included in each area below are a few potential considerations. When planning your career goals it is important to consider whether you'd like to manage large teams or instead focus on a non-manager, specialist/expert role. Set both short- and long-term objectives for financial goals . Finally, with work/life goals, be creative, planning both your time and potential for broader experiences outside the office.

A note for the indecisive: setting goals sooner gives you more time to accomplish them!

Q: What are your career aspiration, financial achievement, and work/life balance goals?

Career-Fit Goals:

Career

- Do I want to get work done through others as a manager, or be a hands-on specialist?
- Do I want to build work for myself?
- Do I want to get deep experience in one industry or get broad experiences across fields?
- Do I want to have lots of responsibility for people and/or products, or maintain a less stressful work life?

Financial

- What do I want my salary to be in two years, five years, ten years?
- How much do I need in my 401k? When?
- What big purchases do I want to be able to afford?

Work/Life Balance

- Typical hours per work week?
- Travel required per month?
- Vacation days per year?
- What do I want to have time for outside of work?

POSITIONED TO FIT: YOUR ONE PAGE PLAN

Having completed the worksheets and planning on the preceding pages, summarize your work in the appropriate boxes below.

Try to capture the core ideas as briefly as possible. This will serve as a one-page reference for you as you plan and make career decisions.

Strengths-Fit

"I am a natural..."

"My essential knowledge and skills are..."

Interests-Fit

"My interests are in..."

Company-Fit

I am looking for the following in a company:

Goals-Fit

My career, financial, and work/life goals are:

SEARCH WORKSHEET: STRENGTHS & INTERESTS

Referencing your "Positioned to Fit" summary on the previous page along with the guidelines on the previous pages, use the worksheet below to indicate the job roles to consider in your job search and career path.

Job Roles – similar to job titles, these are jobs you might apply for across industries.

Job Industries – these are the fields in which a business operates.

Example: Someone might work as an Account Manager in for a company in the pharmaceutical industry.

"Based on my strengths and interests I plan to focus on..."

Job Role	Yes	Maybe	No	Notes
Account Management	☐	☐	☐	
Administrative	☐	☐	☐	
Administering Health Services	☐	☐	☐	
Advertising	☐	☐	☐	
Business Development	☐	☐	☐	
Clerical, Processing	☐	☐	☐	
Creative, Design	☐	☐	☐	
Consulting	☐	☐	☐	
Customer Service, Support	☐	☐	☐	
Distribution	☐	☐	☐	
Education	☐	☐	☐	
Engineering	☐	☐	☐	
Executive Management	☐	☐	☐	
Finance	☐	☐	☐	
Human Resources	☐	☐	☐	
Information Systems/ Technology	☐	☐	☐	
Legal	☐	☐	☐	
Merchandising	☐	☐	☐	
Operations/Production	☐	☐	☐	
Purchasing	☐	☐	☐	
R&D/Scientific	☐	☐	☐	
Research	☐	☐	☐	
Sales	☐	☐	☐	

To apply your "Positioned to Fit" summary (page 53) along with the guidelines on the previous pages, use the worksheet below to indicate the job roles to consider in your job search and career path.

"Based on my strengths and interests, I plan to focus on..."

Job Industry	Yes	Maybe	No
Accounting	☐	☐	☐
Advertising	☐	☐	☐
Aerospace/Aviation/Automotive	☐	☐	☐
Agriculture, Forestry & Fishing	☐	☐	☐
Biotech	☐	☐	☐
Business/Professional Services			
Hospitality	☐	☐	☐
Computer Hardware/Software/Internet	☐	☐	☐
Construction / Home improvement	☐	☐	☐
Consulting	☐	☐	☐
Education	☐	☐	☐
Engineering/Architecture	☐	☐	☐
Entertainment/Recreation	☐	☐	☐
Finance/Banking/Insurance	☐	☐	☐
Food service	☐	☐	☐
Government/Military	☐	☐	☐
Healthcare/Medical	☐	☐	☐
Internet (ASP)	☐	☐	☐
Legal	☐	☐	☐
Manufacturing	☐	☐	☐
Market Research/Marketing/PR	☐	☐	☐
Media/Printing/Publishing	☐	☐	☐

Job Industry	Yes	Maybe	No
Mining	☐	☐	☐
Non-Profit	☐	☐	☐
Pharmaceutical/Chemical	☐	☐	☐
Research/Science	☐	☐	☐
Real Estate	☐	☐	☐
Retail/Wholesale Trade	☐	☐	☐
Telecommunications	☐	☐	☐
Utilities	☐	☐	☐
Wholesale	☐	☐	☐
Transportation/Distribution	☐	☐	☐
Electric, Gas, Sanitary Services	☐	☐	☐

INTERVIEW NOTES

Using the guidance on the previous pages, complete the left side of this worksheet ahead of time.

Company: _____

Job: _____

Interviewer: _____

Notes / Preparation:

My Strengths

My Questions (about the job, company)

Talents

Uncover Strengths Needed
•Strengths of the top people?
•Why people fail?

Knowledge & Skills

Learn about the Company & Goals
Training, career opportunities, supervisor, work/life, etc.

MAKING A DECISION

Company: _____   Notes:

Job: _____

"Does this job fit my..."

Strengths?	Yes	Partially	No	Notes:
Strength 1:	☐	☐	☐	
Strength 2:	☐	☐	☐	
Strength 3:	☐	☐	☐	
Strength 4:	☐	☐	☐	
Strength 5:	☐	☐	☐	

Interests?	Yes	Partially	No	Notes:
Interest 1:	☐	☐	☐	
Interest 2:	☐	☐	☐	
Interest 3:	☐	☐	☐	
Interest 4:	☐	☐	☐	

Goals?	Yes	Partially	No	Notes:
Career:	☐	☐	☐	
Financial:	☐	☐	☐	
Work/Life:	☐	☐	☐	
Other:	☐	☐	☐	

Company Preference?	Yes	Partially	No	Notes:
Health Benefits	☐	☐	☐	
Location/ Commute	☐	☐	☐	
Management	☐	☐	☐	
Training	☐	☐	☐	
Career Opps	☐	☐	☐	
Reputation	☐	☐	☐	
Pay Levels	☐	☐	☐	
Supervisor:	☐	☐	☐	

Total Score (optional):

_____ Yes _____ Partial _____ No

APPENDIX

STRENGTH MATCHING JOB SUGGESTIONS

The Clifton StrengthsFinder™ was created by Dr. Donald O. Clifton of the Gallup Organization, who is considered the Father of Strengths-Based Psychology. Through over 40 years of research, Gallup identified the common talents across their 2+ million person database. For these they named the 34 most common talents and created StrengthsFinder® as an individual identification tool.

For each StrengthsFinder© talent below, you will find the industries, work areas and job titles that the survey respondents who had that talent and indicated they used that talent in their job regularly.

Now, Discover Your Strengths (Free Press) and StrengthsFinder 2.0 (Gallup Press) are excellent books to learn more about strengths and each of the talent themes listed below.

Achiever®

Guideline:	*Look for fast-paced industries and roles that help "Achievers" with their daily need to accomplish something tangible.*
Example Industries:	Healthcare/Medical, Finance/Banking/Insurance, Market Research/Marketing/PR, Technology
Example Work Areas:	Executive Management, Administrative, Strategy, Distribution, Information Systems/Information Technology
Example Jobs:	R&D Manager, Technical Consultant, Director of Portfolio Management, Director of Project Management, Campaign Manager, Marketing Specialist

Activator®

Guideline:	*Look for action-based industries and roles that allow "Activators" to satisfy their need to "get started" on projects quickly.*
Example Industries:	Consulting, Non-Profit, Engineering/Architecture, Manufacturing
Example Work Areas:	Executive Management, Faith-based/Religious, Consulting, Account Management, Sales,
Example Jobs:	Consultant, Pastor, Marketing & Communications Director, Architect, HR Director, Sales Representative

Adaptability®

Guideline:	*Look for industries and roles that allow people with "Adaptability" to live in the moment and feed off the need for spontaneous decision making.*
Example Industries:	Healthcare/Medical, Finance/Banking/Insurance, Market Research/Marketing/PR, Technology
Example Work Areas:	Operations/Production, Engineering, Finance, Administrative, Sales, Education, Account Management
Example Jobs:	Teacher, Principal, Professional Staff Development Director, Chief Strategy Officer, Chef, Transportation Supervisor, Artist

Analytical®

Guideline:	*Look for industries and roles that allow people with "Analytical" to use facts and logic to make decisions.*
Example Industries:	Education, Market Research/Marketing/PR, Food Service, Transportation/Distribution, Media/Print/Publishing, Entertainment/Recreation
Example Work Areas:	Strategy, Operations/Production, Information Systems/Information Technology, Finance, Legal, Engineering/Architecture, R&D/Scientific
Example Jobs:	Accountant, Attorney, Software Architect, Hardware Designer, Project/Interface Engineer, Stock Analyst, Operations Specialist

StrengthsFinder®, Clifton StrengthsFinderTM and each of the 34 CliftonStrengthsFinder theme names are trademarks of The Gallup Organization. For more information visit www.gallup.com

60

STRENGTH MATCHING JOB SUGGESTIONS

Arranger™

Guideline: *industries and roles that allow "Arrangers" to manage multiple variables / projects systematically.*

Example Industries: Hospitality, Finance/Banking/Insurance, Engineering/Architecture, Manufacturing, Technology, Transportation/Distribution, Construction

Example Work Areas: Operations/Production, Finance, Executive Management, Information Systems/Information Technology, Strategy, Engineering/Architecture

Example Jobs: Event Planner, Capital Investment Analyst, Software Developer, Office Manager, Project Engineer, Operations Manager

Belief®

Guideline: *industries and roles that allow people with "Belief" to follow their values. Jobs in Look for fields can be fulfilling despite lower pay/prestige.*

Example Industries: Non-Profit, Education, Healthcare/Medical, Government/Military

Example Work Areas: Education, Administrative, Clerical/Processing, Business Development, Faith-based/Religious, Administering Health and Mental Health Services

Example Jobs: Teacher, Pastor, Personal Assistant, Therapist, Career Coach, Emergency Personnel, Elected Official, Dentist, Social Worker

Command®

Guideline: *Look for industries and roles that give people with "Command" the freedom to exercise their desire to take charge.*

Example Industries: Technology, Retail/Wholesale Trade, Non-Profit, Education, Healthcare/Medical

Example Work Areas: Executive Management, Operations/Production, Education, Faith-based/Religious, Engineering/Architecture, Legal

Example Jobs: CEO, Retail Manager, Pastor, Entrepreneur, Project Manager, Principal, Hospital Director

Communication®

Guideline: *industries and roles that allow people with "Communication" a platform for expressing their thoughts and ideas through stories.*

Example Industries: Media/Printing/Publishing, Education, Business/Professional Services, Consulting, Non-Profit, Market Research/Marketing/PR

Example Work Areas: Creative Design, Education, Customer Service/Support, Sales, Executive Management, Business Development

Example Jobs: Editor, Teacher, HR Director, Consultant, CEO, Pastor, Marketing Specialist

Competition®

Guideline: *industries and roles that give people with "Competition" an opportunity to make competitive comparisons during the course of their day.*

Example Industries: Finance/Banking/Insurance, Advertising, Market Research/Marketing/PR, Business/Professional Services

Example Work Areas: Sales, Executive Management, Advertising, Distribution, Customer Service

Example Jobs: Loan Originator, COO, Account Manager, Sales Director, Chief Strategy Officer

STRENGTH MATCHING JOB SUGGESTIONS

Connectedness®

Guideline:	*industries and roles that give people with "Connectedness" an opportunity to build coordination and teamwork toward a cause or mission.*
Example Industries:	Non-Profit, Education, Consulting, Healthcare/Medical, Government/Military, Entertainment/Recreation
Example Work Areas:	Human Resources, Non-Profit, Faith-based/Religious, Education, Consulting, Administrative
Example Jobs:	Recruiter, Teacher, Pastor, Personal Assistant, Doctor, Elected Official, Community Organizer, Entertainer

Consistency® (also called Fairnesss™)

Guideline:	*industries and roles that provide people with "Consistency" an opportunity to exercise their desire to treat other people fairly.*
Example Industries:	Education, Retail/Wholesale Trade, Food Service, Government/Military, Biotech, Utilities, Non-Profit, Healthcare/Medical
Example Work Areas:	Administrative, Sales, Education, Operations/Production, Customer Service/Support, Legal, Elected Official
Example Jobs:	Principal, Special Education Teacher, Chef, Emergency Personnel, Law Enforcement, Retail Manager, HR Manager

Context®

Guideline:	*industries and roles that give people with "Context" the ability to excel in their positions by framing the current with the past.*
Example Industries:	Healthcare/Medical, Engineering/Architecture, Construction, Technology, Education, Government/Military
Example Work Areas:	Information Systems/Information Technology, Creative Design, Executive Management, Education, Legal, Elected Official
Example Jobs:	Principal, Special Education Teacher, Chef, Emergency Personnel, Law Enforcement, Retail Manager, HR Manager, Service Manager

Deliberative®

Guideline:	*industries and roles that give those with "Deliberative" the opportunity to weigh risks for the benefit of the organization.*
Example Industries:	Finance/Banking/Insurance, Healthcare/Medical, Engineering/Architecture, Government/Military, Utilities, Real Estate
Example Work Areas:	Finance, Insurance, Engineering, Human Resources, Legal, Strategy, Consulting, Executive Management, Analysis
Example Jobs:	Engineer, Architect, Underwriter, Actuary, Lawyer, Project Manager, Operations Manager, HR Manager, Service Manager

Developer®

Guideline:	*industries and roles that give "Developers" the opportunity to focus on drawing out the potential of others in their daily responsibilities.*
Example Industries:	Education, Non-Profit, Hospitality, Entertainment/Recreation, Business/Professional Services, Healthcare/Medical, Government/Military
Example Work Areas:	Human Resources, Executive Management, Education, Customer Service/Support, Faith-based/Religious
Example Jobs:	Training Manager, Teacher, Coach, Pastor, Manager, Physical Therapist, Elected Official

STRENGTH MATCHING JOB SUGGESTIONS

Discipline™

Guideline: *Look for industries and roles that allow those with "Discipline" to follow a relatively predictable schedule and set of outcomes throughout their day.*

Example Industries: Technology, Business/Professional Services, Engineering/Architecture, Transportation/Distribution, Construction, Utilities

Example Work Areas: Administrative, Maintenance, Operations/Production, Information Systems/Information Technology, Engineering, Manufacturing, Consulting

Example Jobs: Personal Assistant, Software Architect, Accountant, Engineer, Architect, Business Process Consultant, Logistics Manager

Empathy™

Guideline: *Look for industries and roles that help those with "Empathy" to succeed by understanding where others are coming from.*

Example Industries: Education, Non-Profit, Healthcare/Medical, Consulting, Retail/Wholesale Trade, Government/Military, Advertising

Example Work Areas: Education, Human Resources, Administrative, Customer Service/Customer Support, Legal, Sales

Example Jobs: Teacher, HR Manager, Manager, Personal Assistant, Customer Support Specialist, Lawyer, Outside Sales Representative

Fairness™ (also called Consistency®)

Guideline: *Look for industries and roles that provide people with "Consistency" an opportunity to exercise their desire to treat other people fairly.*

Example Industries: Education, Retail/Wholesale Trade, Food Service, Government/Military, Biotech, Utilities, Non-Profit, Healthcare/Medical

Example Work Areas: Administrative, Sales, Education, Operations/Production, Customer Service/Support, Legal, Elected Official

Example Jobs: Principal, Special Education Teacher, Chef, Emergency Personnel, Law Enforcement, Retail Manager, HR Manager

Focus™

Guideline: *Look for roles that provide those with "Focus" a degree of independence/autonomy and rewards their ability to be effieciency with efforts.*

Example Industries: Finance/Banking/Insurance, Utilities, Transportation/Distribution, Agriculture/Forestry/Fishing, Biotech, Media/Print/Publishing

Example Work Areas: Sales, Executive Management, Information Systems/Information Technology, Engineering, Manufacturing, Consulting, Research, Distribution

Example Jobs: Sales Representative, CEO, Software Architect, Engineer, Operations Manager, Technical Production Specialist, Research Analyst, Procurement Manager

Futuristic®

Guideline: *Look for industries and roles that give people with "Futuristic" a platform for casting a vision of the future for the benefit of the organization.*

Example Industries: Non-Profit, Consulting, Hospitality, Aerospace/Aviation/Automotive, Market Research/Marketing/PR, Advertising

Example Work Areas: Executive Management, Business Development, Consulting, Analysis, Faith-based/Religious, Sales

Example Jobs: CEO, Pastor, Director - Business Development, Management Consultant, Equity Research Analyst, Outside Sales Manager

STRENGTH MATCHING JOB SUGGESTIONS

Harmony®

Guideline: *Look for roles that give people with "Harmony" a supportive work environment and opportunities to find consensus.*

Example Industries: Education, Non-Profit, Finance/Banking/Insurance, Retail/Wholesale Trade, Market Research/Marketing/PR, Healthcare/Medical

Example Work Areas: Education, Sales, Administrative, Finance, Human Resources, Account Management

Example Jobs: Teacher, Sales Representative, Administrative Assistant, Banker, HR Manager, Account Representative

Ideation®

Guideline: *Look for industries and roles that allow those with "Ideation" to use their ability to connect the dots and innovate in a beneficial way.*

Example Industries: Consulting, Manufacturing, Education, Technology, Research/Science, Entertainment/Recreation, Advertising, Finance/Banking/Insurance

Example Work Areas: Executive Management, Business Development, Education, Creative/Design, Consulting, Advertising

Example Jobs: Management Consultant, Process Engineer, Training Manager, Web/Software Developer, Research Scientist, Writer, Designer, Investment Banker

Includer®

Guideline: *Look for industries and roles that provide "Includers" with the opportunity to exercise their desire to bring everyone into involvement in their jobs.*

Example Industries: Education, Healthcare/Medical, Non-Profit, Finance/Banking/Insurance, Consulting, Government/Military

Example Work Areas: Education, Strategy, Administering Health and Mental Health Services, Sales, Faith-based/Religious, Administrative, HR Manager, Legal

Example Jobs: Teacher, Training Manager, Lawyer, Doctor, Pastor, Insurance Agent, Loan Officer, Elected Official

Individualization®

Guideline: *Look for industries and roles that give those with "Individualization" a productive format for identifying the unique qualities in the people they contact.*

Example Industries: Healthcare/Medical, Retail/Wholesale Trade, Hospitality, Construction/Home Improvement

Example Work Areas: Human Resources, Executive Management, Customer Service/Support, Consulting, Administering Health and Mental Health Services

Example Jobs: Doctor, HR Representative, Retail Manager, Customer Support Specialist, Consultant, Nurse

Input®

Guideline: *Look for industries and roles that provide a framework for those with "Input" to use their desire to collect information as part of their job.*

Example Industries: Education, Business/Professional Services, Legal, Healthcare/Medical, Research/Science, Real Estate

Example Work Areas: Education, Consulting, Administering Health and Mental Health Services, Legal, Research, Real Estate

Example Jobs: Professor, Tax Consultant, Medical Researcher, Scientist, Lawyer, Market Research Analyst, Real Estate Analyst

STRENGTH MATCHING JOB SUGGESTIONS

Intellection®

Guideline: *Look for industries and roles that allow those with "Intellection" to focus inwardly at work and enjoy contemplating their thoughts.*

Example Industries: Technology, Consulting, Healthcare/Medical, Market Research/Marketing/PR, Engineering/Architecture, Aerospace/Aviation/Automotive

Example Work Areas: Information Systems/Information Technology, Finance, R&D/Scientific, Research, Legal, Taxation, Healthcare, Strategy

Example Jobs: Software Architect, Actuary, Financial Analyst, Research Analyst, Scientist, Physicist, Lawyer, Pharmaceutical Research

Learner®

Guideline: *Look for knowledge-intense industries and roles that give "Learners" the ability to look at new information on a regular basis to perform well.*

Example Industries: Education, Technology, Healthcare/Medical, Pharmaceutical/Chemical, Research/Science, Aerospace/Aviation/Automotive

Example Work Areas: Education, Consulting, Information Systems/Information Technology, R&D/Scientific, Research, Legal, Taxation, Healthcare, Strategy

Example Jobs: College Professor, Management Consultant, Product Developer, Research Analyst, Lawyer, State and Local Tax Specialist, Scientist

Maximizer®

Guideline: *Look for industries and roles that provide "Maximizers" frequent opportunities to take the status quo and make improvements with both people and processes.*

Example Industries: Education, Consulting, Non-Profit, Healthcare/Medical, Business/Professional Services, Manufacturing, Utilities

Example Work Areas: Education, Consulting, Human Resources, Executive Management, Faith-based/Religious, Strategy, Business Development, Creative/Design, Advertising

Example Jobs: Teacher, Strategy Consultant, Training Manager, Chief Operating Officer, Pastor, Business Development Director, Product Designer, Creative Artist

Positivity®

Guideline: *Look for industries and roles that provide avenues for people with "Positivity" to highlight and focus on the positive in their jobs.*

Example Industries: Education, Business/Professional Services, Consulting, Healthcare/Medical, Non-Profit, Media/Printing/Publishing, Advertising, Government/Military

Example Work Areas: Education, Executive Management, Human Resources, Sales, Customer Support/Customer Service, Business Development, Consulting

Example Jobs: Teacher, Recruiter, Flight Attendant, Chief Marketing Officer, Business Development Director, Psychologist, Pastor, Outside Sales Representative

Relator®

Guideline: *Look for industries and roles that can allow "Relators" time to develop deep relationships as part of their responsibilities.*

Example Industries: Finance/Banking/Insurance, Consulting, Government/Military, Manufacturing, Entertainment/Recreation

Example Work Areas: Human Resources, Administrative, Executive Management, Information Systems/Information Technology, Finance, Legal, Advertising

Example Jobs: HR Manager, Executive Assistant, CEO, Information Technology Manager, Accounting Manager, Lawyer, Account Manager

StrengthsFinder®, Clifton StrengthsFinderTM and each of the 34 CliftonStrengthsFinder theme names are trademarks of The Gallup Organization. For more information visit www.gallup.com

STRENGTH MATCHING JOB SUGGESTIONS

Responsibility®

Guideline:
Look for industries and roles that benefit from someone with "Responsibility" as that person has a deep conviction to follow through on their commitments.

Example Industries:
Finance/Banking/Insurance, Healthcare/Medical, Retail/Wholesale Trade, Government/Military, Pharmaceutical/Chemical, Transportation/Distribution

Example Work Areas:
Operations/Production, Sales, Administrative, Finance, Information Systems/Information Technology, Distribution, Maintenance, Legal

Example Jobs:
Operations Manager, Sales Representative, Executive Assistant, Loan Officer, IT Manager, Accountant, Logistics Manager, Facilities Manager, Lawyer

Restorative®

Guideline:
Look for industries and roles that give people with "Restorative" the opportunity to solve problems as part of their responsibilities on a regular basis.

Example Industries:
Finance/Banking/Insurance, Retail/Wholesale Trade, Healthcare/Medical, Aerospace/Aviation/Automotive, Engineering/Architecture

Example Work Areas:
Customer Service/Support, R&D/Scientific, Manufacturing, Account Management, Information Systems/Information Technology, Operations/Production

Example Jobs:
Actuary, Retail Manager, Doctor, Aerospace Engineer, Mechanic, Structural Engineer, Account Manager, Process Engineer, IT Manager

Self-Assurance®

Guideline:
Look for industries and roles that provide those with "Self-Assurance" a platform for exercising their self-confidence as a function of their job.

Example Industries:
Business/Professional Services, Technology, Consulting, Finance/Banking/Insurance, Healthcare/Medical, Government/Military

Example Work Areas:
Executive Management, Operations/Production, Government/Military, Engineering, R&D/Scientific, Account Management, Business Development

Example Jobs:
CFO, Consultant, Accountant, Lawyer, Actuary, IT Manager, Elected Official, Armed Services Officer, Scientist, Engineer, Relationship Manager

Significance®

Guideline:
Look for industries and roles that give those with "Significance" an opportunity to be recognized as well as surround themselves with successful people.

Example Industries:
Business/Professional Services, Government/Military, Engineering/Architecture, Research/Science, Media/Printing/Publishing, Entertainment/Recreation

Example Work Areas:
Executive Management, Sales, Business Development, Consulting, Legal, R&D/Scientific, Government/Military, Research, Creative/Design, Manufacturing

Example Jobs:
CEO, Outside Sales Rep., Business Development Coordinator, Management Consultant, Trial Lawyer, Laboratory Research Analyst, Elected Official

Strategic™

Guideline:
Look for industries and roles that utilize the perspectives of those with "Strategic" in a typical job by presenting problems that can be solved by many scenarios.

Example Industries:
Consulting, Technology, Government/Military, Manufacturing, Entertainment/Recreation, Aerospace/Aviation/Automotive, Advertising

Example Work Areas:
Consulting, Executive Management, Human Resources, Business Development, Strategy, Manufacturing, Operations/Production, Engineering, Legal

Example Jobs:
Strategy Consultant, CEO, Armed Services General, Military Agent, Tax Lawyer, Computer Programmer, Financial Engineer

Woo®

Guideline:
Look for industries and roles that give "Woos" the opportunity to use their desire to meet and connect with new people on a regular basis in their job.

Example Industries:
Consulting, Healthcare/Medical, Finance/Banking/Insurance, Business/Professional Services, Non-Profit, Government/Military, Food Service

Example Work Areas:
Human Resources, Consulting, Sales, Executive Management, Customer Service/Support, Business Development

Example Jobs:
Recruiter, Consultant, Outside Sales Rep., Family Doctor, Pharmaceutical Sales Rep., CEO, Customer Support Specialist

RESEARCH METHODOLOGY

In the summer of 2011 visitors of strengthstest.com were invited to participate in an survey regarding their strengths and job fit. The survey asked 47 questions grouped into job profile, work experience, strengths, interests, goals, intent to stay in the job, work performance, satisfaction levels, as well as demographic details. Responses of the participants were analyzed based on fit factors, type of work, history, experience and performance levels.

Fit levels were measured across a group of questions, each on a seven point scale. For example, company-fit included assessment of things such as the individuals' compensation, manager, benefits, and training opportunities. High-fit respondents are those with an average of 6.3 or greater across the set of "fit" questions and low-fit have an average of 4 or lower.

There were 789 respondents from over 50 countries and 32 industries.

RECOMMENDED READING

To view these recommendations online, visit www.TheFitFactors.com/reading

Strengths Focused:

Now, Discover Your Strengths
by Marcus Buckingham and Donald Clifton (Free Press, 2001)
This is the first strengths-focused book by Gallup and the most comprehensive on the topic from Gallup. Includes reference materials in the book as well.

Strengths Based Selling
by Tony Rutigliano and Brian Brim (Gallup Press, 2010)
This helps you understand how to apply your Clifton StrengthsFinder™ themes in a sales position.

Management and Leadership Focused:

First, Break All the Rules
by Marcus Buckingham and Curt Coffman (Simon & Schuster, 1999)
This is a great book for anyone in a management position. The research of the Gallup Organization revealed 12 key elements that every manager needs to focus on to engage their teams. One of the findings in this book led to the StrengthsFinder® assessment and subsequent books.

Strengths-Based Leadership
by Tom Rath and Barry Conchie (Gallup Press, 2009)
For those in leadership and management positions, this book helps you understand how your strengths help you lead, build a team and motivate others.

Job Search Focused:

What Color Is Your Parachute? Job Hunter's Workbook
by Richard Nelson Bolles (Ten Speed Press, 2010)
The is the workbook companion to the the primary book *What Color Is Your Parachute?* The workbook is a manageable 64 pages, compared to the sometimes overwhelming 384 page primary book.

ABOUT THE AUTHOR

Brad Pugh is a consultant on human capital, workforce strategy, and individual career planning.

Brad has spent his career as an entrepreneur and business consultant in both private and public corporations, dedicating his time within those roles to coaching individuals and managers on the best practices associated with building great careers for themselves and their team members.

He has conducted over 1,500 human resources consultation sessions with senior executives at Fortune 500 companies and international government entities throughout the US and Asia. His work has focused on talent management (including recruitment, leadership and employee development), strategy execution, sales optimization, and organization design. Brad has also conducted workshops and delivered training presentations to teams at organizations including Microsoft, National Grid, Allstate, Procter & Gamble, Starbucks, the Government of Canada, the Coca-Cola Company, Tupperware, National Instruments and GlaxoSmithKline. He is currently focused on talent challenges in Asia, spending his time in Singapore, Hong Kong, Shanghai and Beijing.

Prior to his consulting role, Brad was a leader and founder of several software and e-commerce firms. In these companies, he oversaw the creation of products for customers and achieved the sale of two of these business ventures. Brad began his career at Oracle Corp.

Brad can be reached at brad@thefitfactors.com.

Made in the USA
Lexington, KY
05 May 2014